THE WAYCARD ORACLE

A Guide to the Inner Journey

Martha Winona Travers, PhD

Schiffer Publishing Ltd

4880 Lower Valley Road • Atglen, PA 19310

To John Charles and Paul Michael,
that you may feel the Radiance in your lives
and live with great Joyfulness.

Library of Congress Control Number: 2016930179

Type set in Mai Pro

ISBN: 978-0-7643-5059-7
Printed in China

Published by Schiffer Publishing, Ltd.
4880 Lower Valley Road
Atglen, PA 19310
Phone: (610) 593-1777; Fax: (610) 593-2002
E-mail: Info@schifferbooks.com

ACKNOWLEDGMENTS

As with all moments in life, this expression of the Way would not have been possible without the assistance of many guides, friends, and nurturers. Gratitude to the five elements: Radiance, Air, Fire, Water, and Earth for my being. Gratitude to my elders, both familial and spiritual, especially to my parents, John Wesley Goff and Ruth MacLaren Goff, and to my teachers, Cheryl Stereff and Alberto Taxo. Gratitude to my sisters Elizabeth, Diane, and Linda for many years of support; to my sons John and Paul for their wisdom and patience; to their father, Michael E. Stoner, builder of houses and protector of pilgrims; and to Michael's parents, Charles and Marie Stoner, beloved ones.

Many friends have contributed guidance and support to me on my spiritual path. I am especially grateful for the assistance of Linda Abrahamowicz, Laura Deschaines, Ed Engle, Carrie Beth Monette, Vera Lucia Moura, Laurie DeLoof Pruitt, John Reimanis, Ed Sarath, Lynne Serfling, Kim Alison Sanwald, and Mikkal Smith.

Special thanks, as well, to Erin McAuley at Impluvium Studios (impluviumstudios.com) for her expert skill in rendering my card design in physical form and to the editors and staff at Schiffer Books.

I have been significantly assisted in my ability to conceptualize the Way by all of the texts listed in the bibliography but especially by the work of Doug Boyd, Joseph Campbell, Joan Halifax, P. L. Travers, and Lao Tzu. Gratitude to Liz and Colin Murray whose *Celtic Tree Oracle* taught me the power of divination. And to all my beloved students, "Namaste."

Finally, this book would not have been possible without the land on which I have lived or where I have spent time in retreat during the many years of writing and revising this work. Immense gratitude to Duirhaven, the home in the woods where I lived between 1989 and 2005, to Pearl House where I now live, and to the GilChrist retreat center where I have been given solitude and serenity on individual retreats over a period of seventeen years. Thank you to John Howie, whose stewardship of the land at GilChrist has created sacred space for many pilgrims on the path, to Deborah Yeager whose warm heart and generous spirit nurtured many of those pilgrims, and to Rob Lehman and Molly Vass-Lehman whose vision created GilChrist.

"The months and days are wayfarers
of a hundred generations,
and the years that come
and go are also travelers."

—Matsuo Basho[1]

CONTENTS

FOREWORD

In an ever-changing world, it is in our best interest, from time to time, to seek guidance and inspiration from sources beyond our current knowledge or understanding. Since ancient times, people have used oracles to assist them in seeing beyond their own limited perspectives. The history of oracle use is of ancient and archaic shamanic origins. As part of their survival strategy, indigenous peoples used a wide variety of oracle forms, from reading the patterns in clouds and birds to interpreting patterns on the shells of turtles and in the movement of water. They were great observers of natural patterns, of shifts in the landscapes without, and of changes in the interior climate within.

Taoist scholars tell us that this practice is the foundation of the *I Ching*, the Chinese *Book of Changes*, which is perhaps the world's most famous oracle and has continued to be in use for millennia.

In modern times, C. G. Jung, the great pioneer of depth psychology, crafted a powerful psychological theory that placed the sacred at the very heart of inquiry. Jung referred to the "archetypal self," as the source most likely to help a person acquire a transcendent perspective. This "Tao of the heart" helps us navigate life by coming into harmonious relationship with it. Dr. Jung knew that we also need practical techniques to help us access the sources of greater wisdom. Jung turned to astrology, the *I Ching*, and the technique of "active imagination," which he developed, to guide his clients in the process of individuation. For Jung, whenever a new situation or challenge presents itself, be it a time of change, crisis, or transition, or a time when one feels stuck in a circumstance or self-defeating pattern, it is necessary to transcend one's own, and inevitably, limited point of view.

To do so requires a skillful practice such as divination, the consulting of oracles. Etymologically speaking, "divination" suggests "seeking divine guidance." Because of its sacred nature, Jung believed a person should prepare themselves before seeking guidance from the oracle. This preparation could take a variety of forms but included practices such as solitude and fasting, which help a person loosen the hold of ego that otherwise might cause one to project one's own fantasies while consulting the oracle and thereby to lose the opportunity of receiving a transcendentally wise perspective from a greater source of knowing.

In those indigenous cultures today where dream and mythology are still alive and where the heart is open, the capacity to feel intuitively is still well-developed and, thus, divination is still very much at the heart of navigating life. When needing insight or guidance, a person utilizing divination steps into the numinous world of the archetypal imagination where they can perceive patterns and possibilities. Those who follow this path know that the divine depth of the cosmos is intelligent and wise and is sketching patterns for their next steps, one at a time. A crisis may be an opportunity for healing, expansion, or needed awareness. Therefore, knowing how to reflect on and interpret the oracle is a necessary skill. Doing so invites reflective and soulful moments which often precede important existential choices.

In *The WayCard Oracle*, we have a new and elegantly profound text, rich with wisdom, that can be read contemplatively on its own whether or not one wishes to consult the oracle cards. This book has the feel of the Taoist profundity of the *I Ching*. Without all the arcane detail of the Chinese oracle that can overwhelm the newcomer, *The WayCard Oracle* is organized around the various, basic archetypal situations of life that are named with Way-pointing Arrows on the cards themselves. These themes—Child, Nest, Hero, Crossroads, Threshold, Betrayal, Earth, Air, Fire, and Water—reflect the archetypal hero journey, the elemental forces of life, and the fundamental situations any of us can find ourselves encountering in our life journey.

In this oracle, Martha Winona Travers draws from a lifetime of accumulated wisdom and reflection. Her book is thoroughly researched and is crafted and made accessible for anyone in our time who might be seeking a way forward or simply a way to be in any situation that may arise. Therapists and Jungian analysts will find this oracle to be a practical tool that can be used in consultation with clients to assist them in gaining a broader understanding of their inner life and outer journey. As a Jungian psychologist and shamanic teacher with more than three decades of experience working with clients and divination, I know *The WayCard Oracle* will help you identify energy clusters, or archetypes, that are presently active and influencing emotions, thoughts, and actions.

Martha writes in a profoundly gentle, poetic style with an implicitly spiritual voice. She has deep roots in the wisdom tradition of Taoist-Chinese principles and has long been a student of the High Andean-Kichwa philosophy of walking a heart-open and earth-honoring path. On this path, everything is alive and infused with sentience, intelligence, and power. I have walked alongside her on this path as a very good friend and am pleased that others will now have an opportunity to experience her guidance.

—**C. Michael Smith**, PhD
Jungian Psychologist and author of *Jung and Shamanism in Dialogue* and of *Psychotherapy and the Sacred*
Crow's Nest

PREFACE

The WayCard Oracle began on a small island in the Caribbean in the winter of 1995. The previous fall, I had undergone emergency surgery, and while under anesthetic, all my vital signs had stopped. My body "re-booted" itself before the attending physicians had to take any action. It was an odd and unaccounted-for event. Other than that sudden pause, the surgery went smoothly. Upon return to my daily life, however, I began to notice a significant increase in intuitive moments—knowing that the phone would ring before it rang, knowing who it was who was calling, anticipating comments a person would make, knowing when to slow the car as I drove country roads at night, avoiding a deer that would then become visible, and dreaming of events that later took place.

I had traveled to the island of St. Kitts with a friend and a group of people I had never met. I had never been to the Caribbean before, and I was amazed by the incredible beauty of the island flora, the ocean surrounding us, and the warm-hearted islanders. Something about the island aura caused a small group of us to become close more rapidly than might happen in the cold north from which we came. I had recently begun to do divination using a beautiful card deck created by Liz and Colin Murray: *The Celtic Tree Oracle*. I felt a desire to do some divination for two of the women I had met on the island, but had not brought the card deck with me.

Immediately upon recognizing this desire and regretting that I had no oracle deck, I heard an intuitive voice say, "You can make your own deck." I felt the truth of this insight, and that afternoon, when the sun was at its most intense, I retreated to my small room where the water of the bay came up to the little cement porch beyond the sliding glass door. Sheer, white, floor-length curtains with small crescent moons embroidered throughout the fabric floated in the open doorway. As the island breeze gently blew the curtains into the room and called them back out of the room, and as the bay water lapped the cement porch, I created thirteen cards on notepaper I had brought with me.

All I had to do was listen and each name of the card was revealed. That evening I gave readings to the two women I had met on the island. When I returned from the island to the northern United States, winter had blanketed the woods where I lived with many inches of white. Sitting in my study on the second story of my home where towering oak trees, still holding many browned leaves, stood quietly outside my windows, I continued to create this new deck of cards. Somehow, I knew precisely which energies needed to be represented in the cards. There was no "hard work," no effort to perceive. Over a period of several days, each card name came into my awareness.

One morning, I received the last card. I knew it was the last card simply because I sensed a strong feeling of completion. When I gathered the cards together and counted them, there were thirty-three cards. I felt a strong affirmation because of the numerological significance of the number 33—the number of spiritual completion.

Since that time, I have given many readings of the cards, and clients have often expressed a desire for their own deck of WayCards. Now, in right timing, that is possible. May all who encounter the WayCards receive deep guidance on their spiritual path. Chashna Cachun!

—**Martha Winona**
GilChrist, 2016

INTRODUCTION

Each of us is a traveler, walking our life path. Through walking our life path, we discover the Way. The Way is TAO. Knowing the Way (TAO) is wisdom.

This journey that we call life is a great teacher. This teacher leads us to our interior so that we may find our Way. In order to see what lies outside with clarity, we must see what lies insides with clarity. The journey to the interior mingles pain and joy. Both experiences illuminate the Way.

As we grow older, our many years of walking give us perspective. We come to realize that there are no wrong turns on the life path. Everything that happens—every decision, every accident, every error—is the path. Each step teaches. All steps help us discover the Way.

We do not know why, sometimes, we must descend into dark places, but we must. We do not know how, suddenly, we ascend, but we do. Gradually, we learn to trust.

You hold in your hands an oracle based on the archetypal patterns of ancient myths and fairy tales and also on the wisdom traditions of earth-honoring peoples. When used in a sacred manner, *The WayCard Oracle* reveals hidden knowledge about your journey and helps you travel more lightly.

As you work with the cards, gradually, you will begin to perceive how all events, emotions, and thoughts have a place in your unfolding journey and belong in your life path. This perception brings acceptance. You will learn to go forward with courage, and your ability to go with the flow of your life will strengthen.

Over time, you will experience the inner peace that comes from knowing that everything must be as it is in order for you to know your Way.

The Philosopher's Stone

Each card in the deck represents a place on the life path, a stage in our journey. Thus, each card can be experienced as a stepping stone—a place to stand, to be still, to listen, and to perceive.

When we stand on an individual stone, we are standing at that stage of life. Each stone, or stage of life, possesses great value—a quality of presence and wisdom unique to that stone. When we pause on the stone and when we gaze at the stone, the hidden gem inherent in that stone is revealed.

When experienced fully, each stepping stone becomes a philosopher's stone—that magical energy sought by the alchemists. In alchemy, the philosopher's stone is a force. This force is a power that transmutes base metal into gold. On the life path, the philosopher's stone is the power of recognition—what the Greek tragedians called "peripetea"—that moment when the hero or heroine sees himself or herself and his or her actions with great clarity. This clarity of recognition acts as a force of transformation in our lives, revealing that nothing in earthly existence is base. Rightly understood, everything is gold.

As you come to know the cards, you begin to recognize the significance of your day-to-day experiences. Hidden in the mundane, you discover gems that glow. Your understanding deepens. The more completely you open yourself to the stone—to each unique stage of life with its multi-faceted experiences—the more profound becomes your understanding. With greater understanding, you hold a key that unlocks a door that before was invisible to you, and the Way opens. This is why the stones are also called "keys."

TABLE OF CORRESPONDENCES

STONE	WAYCARD
Radiance	Divine Light.
Air	Spiritual Inspiration.
Fire	Energetic Catalyst and Transformer.
Water	Healer. Fertility. Beginning of Material Manifestation.
Earth	Manifestation.
Child	Vulnerability. Playfulness. Creativity. Innocence.
Nest	Home. Safety. Security.
Hero/Heroine	The Traveler. The Wayfarer. Courage.
Travel	The Way. Pilgrimage. The Call. The Unknown.
Willingness	A State of Mind. A Condition of Heart.
Force/Ego	The Personality in this Lifetime.
Threshold	The Space Between Worlds.
Seduction	Mystery. Allure. Excitement. Trickery.
Betrayal/Chasm	Fear. Confusion in the Mind and Emotions.
Tears/Grieving	Sorrow. Loss. Expression of Emotion.
Judge	Inner Critic. The Powers of Discrimination and Discernment.
Crossroads	Many Options. Many Roads; One Path.
Silence	Spaciousness. Freedom. A Quiet Mind.
Old Knowledge	Oral and Written Traditions. Runes. Wisdom.
The Inner Door	Initiation. Entering the Mysteries.
Letting Go	Release. Acceptance. Ease.
Faith	Grace. Trust. Certainty. Inner Peace.
Focus	"Thought is a living force."
Gratitude	Recognition of Blessings. Feeling Thanksgiving in the Heart.
Forgiveness	A New Level of Perception.
Love	An Opening of the Heart. Warmth.
Reciprocity	Giving and Receiving. Flow.
The Lover	An Ideal. The Beloved. A Soul Mate.
Laughter/Joy	Great Joy from Deep Within, Not Dependent on the Material World.
Dance/The Body	Physical Expression. Physical Harmony. Fully Incarnated.
Sing/The Voice	Giving One's Gift to the World.
The Wise One	The Grey Ancient. Grandmother. Merlin.
Return	Returning to the Community with Wisdom to Share. Rebirth.

HOW TO USE THE CARDS

A Sacred Practice

When working with *The WayCard Oracle*, you are entering a sacred ceremony. It is important that you approach the cards with reverence. This means setting aside a special time for yourself to consult the cards in a place where you will not be interrupted.

At the beginning of the reading, set up a mesa or altar for the reading. This can be either indoors or outdoors. The mesa or altar can be very simple. Bring each of the five elements to the mesa or altar.

If you are indoors, bring a candle (fire), a feather (air), a bowl of water (water), and a plant (earth) to the area where you will be laying the cards. In doing so, you are connecting with and activating the elemental energies of Air, Fire, Water, and Earth. When you give thanks to these elemental forces, the fifth element—the spiritual element—is activated.

If you are outdoors, go to a place where you can feel the sunlight, the air, the water, and the plants. Listen to the birds. Give thanks to these elemental forces, remembering that this act of thanksgiving opens your consciousness to receive the Divine flow.

When you are ready to begin the reading, light the candle and sit quietly in meditation. Inhale deeply and exhale slowly, giving thanks for your life.

Doing a Reading

When doing a reading for yourself or someone else, trust your own way of working with the cards. The interpretation I give for each card is a starting place for your own insights. Use these interpretations as guides, not as absolutes.

Similarly, the patterns I suggest below are patterns that I use with my clients, but these are not the only patterns possible. Unique patterns will emerge out of your own deep knowing.

Patterns

Five Card

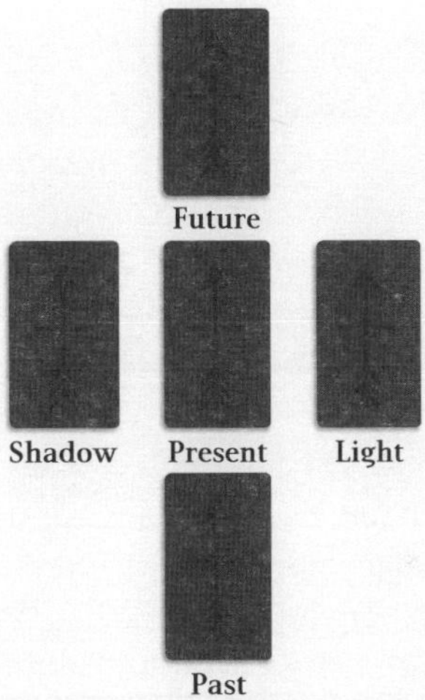

The five-card pattern provides an overview of:

Present: your current situation

Past: shows the energy, attitude, or circumstance that led up to the current situation

Future: suggests the general direction in which the current situation is heading

Shadow: shows energies that are hidden

Light: energies that are direct (light)

This is often a good pattern to use at the beginning of a reading when you want to get a feeling for the context in which you are operating.

To conduct the five-card lay, pick up the cards, close your eyes, inhale deeply, and exhale slowly. Sit quietly for a few moments, letting go of linear thinking while shuffling the cards in your hands. Do not look at the cards while you are shuffling. Sit quietly, feeling and seeing your life path at the present time.

Allow a feeling or image of the present time to come into your awareness. You are not thinking, worrying, wondering, or analyzing. You are not "trying hard." You are resting quietly, allowing yourself to flow and be open. You are feeling and seeing the general ambience—the color, tone, shape—of this phase of your life.

When you feel ready, place the cards on the mesa or altar and spread them in a fan shape with the arrow side of the cards visible and all cards accessible. Keeping your awareness in the feeling of your life path at the present time, select one of the cards to represent the present, but do not turn it over. Place this first card in the central position (present) of the five-card pattern (see diagram).

Continue in this fashion for the other four cards, sitting quietly and feeling each quality. After drawing a card for the present, draw a card for the past, then the future, then what lies in shadow, and finally what lies in light. Place the cards in the pattern indicated in the diagram—all face down so you see the arrow but not the word or words on the face of the card.

Once you have placed all five cards, turn them over, one by one, beginning with the past card. Open the cards following the chronology of past, then present, then future. Turn over the shadow card fourth and the light card last.

With each card, pause once you have turned the card over, and become aware that this card is a stepping stone and a key. Reflect and receive insight before moving to the next card. Allow the word(s) on the card to penetrate your awareness. Notice the associations that come immediately to mind and any emotions or sensations that are stimulated by the card. You may wish to write your first impressions and insights in a journal before turning to the interpretations in this book. The more deeply you encounter each card or stepping stone, the greater your understanding and acceptance of each experience of your life will be.

The shadow and light positions refer to the degree to which an energy is obscured or visible in our lives. Cards that appear in the shadow position indicate a quality or force that is affecting us without our awareness. Sometimes, not only are shadow energies less apparent, they may also be difficult to access when we do become aware of them, and may require careful thought and attention to fully integrate. Cards that appear in the light position indicate a quality or force that is readily available to us. Often we are aware of this quality and are actively incorporating it into our lives. The light energy is easily integrated simply by consciously availing ourselves of its power.

Three Card

The three-card pattern is useful when you have a specific question to ask the cards. Again, sit quietly with eyes closed and shuffle the cards. Inhale deeply and exhale slowly. Still with the eyes closed, allow the question or issue you wish to learn about to arise in your awareness. Take time to become as clear and focused as you can before laying any cards. It is good to narrow the issue and focus your question. Sometimes the journal is useful for this. It can be very helpful to write out the question as precisely as you can articulate it in your journal.

When you have your question clearly phrased, keep the exact words of the question in mind while you lay three cards face down with the arrow visible. Lay the cards left to right in the order you select them without turning them over. Once you have drawn all three cards, begin reading the cards by turning the cards over in the same order that you laid them down and pause between each card to reflect.

One Card

The one-card pattern can be very helpful when you want a single, focused response to a question. The one-card lay is also a good way to select a focus for one's day. Turning a card over in the morning or before sleep at night can act as a stimulus to reflection, insight, and setting intention.

Multi Card

I have worked with clients who enjoy using all the cards in the deck in large, flowing patterns in a single reading. You are encouraged to play with the cards, following your own sense of the Way.

Yes/No Questions

The cards do not answer "yes/no" questions. That is, there is no card with the word "yes" on it and no card with the word "no." However, you can still receive insight regarding an either/or situation by rephrasing your question. Rather than asking, "Should I_____?" ask, "What would be the result if I were to_____?" or "What would be the result if I do not_____?"

INTERPRETATION *of the* WAYCARDS

The WayCards represent spiritual and elemental forces, emotions, attitudes, events, actions, and archetypal structures of the psyche.

There is a natural order, or inherent pattern, in the cards, which is the universal journey of human life from its origin in the numinous realm that defies all naming through incarnation and life on the physical plane with its many upsets, joys, and transformations, to the time of our return to the numinous.

The WayCards depict the stepping stones of this life-journey and, in so doing, they describe not a linear trajectory but a circular rhythm, like the mythical uroborus—the snake wound in a circle with its tail in its mouth. The uroborus is the symbol of the spiritual journey of the soul. That journey forms a circle with no beginning and no end. So it is said: "In the beginning lies the end; in the end, the beginning."

Because writing and speaking are linear modes, the following description of the cards and their meanings is written in a linear manner—from the beginning of this incarnation in physical body to the time we leave our bodies and return to the source. As you use the cards, keep in mind the truth that this life is a circle. Every stepping stone issues from the Radiance and returns to the Radiance to be re-made.

As you work with the cards, you naturally will draw cards "out of order." For example, you may encounter the stepping stone of the Child in the present while finding the Grey Ancient in the past, or you may encounter a new Threshold after achieving a Return to the community. This non-linear aspect of every reading is a reflection of the esoteric, non-linear level of spiritual meaning in our lives.

RADIANCE

The Void. Light coming forth out of darkness.
The raying forth of Divine luminosity.
Bliss. Ecstasy. Enlightenment.

"Our birth is but a sleep and a forgetting:
The Soul that rises with us, our life's Star,
Hath had elsewhere its setting,
And cometh from afar:"
—**William Wordsworth**[1]

Radiance is the primordial state—the a priori, necessary, precondition of the Cosmos. It is "nothing-ness" out of which "being-ness" comes. It is the void. It is the origin of All and is beyond naming. We call it God, Yahweh, Allah, Tao, Ushai, Cosmos. Though we seek to compass it with names, the finite human mind cannot fathom its nature. It is the infinite.

All spiritual traditions, as well as modern, cosmological science, seek to know this primordial state. While the human mind can never know it completely, because all that exists has been birthed from this primordial state and returns to it, our essence can feel/sense/intuit aspects of this primordial condition.

When you pull the Radiance card, you are being reminded that in all circumstances, no matter how small or large, smooth or difficult, there is light as well as darkness. The Radiance card reminds you to trust your present circumstances and to allow your own radiance to shine forth. Radiance emphasizes that you are in bliss now even though your mind may not see this. We can never fall out of the creation; it is impossible. We are the Radiance.

To increase your awareness of the quality of Radiance in your life, you can conduct a ceremonial practice of absorbing the first light at dawn. Stand quietly while the sun rises, gazing at the first glow that appears. As you gaze, inhale deeply, absorbing the gentle glow. As the sun rises and the light becomes too bright for human eyes, look about the creation. We can absorb radiance from the beauty of flowers, butterflies, and other radiant beings. Absorb the beauty around you with your eyes. Use the breath to help you absorb the beauty, inhaling as you gaze.

"The more beauty you absorb;
The more beauty you have to reflect."
—**Eileen Caddy**[2]

AIR

Eyrie. Eagle. Mountain Peaks.
High Altitudes. Spaciousness. Inspiration.
Divine Breath. Wind. Breezes. Caresses.
Freedom. New Beginnings.

"Who can break from the snare of the world
And sit with me among the white clouds?"
—**Han-shan**[3]

Air carries the primordial Radiance to Earth. Air is the wind of inspiration, filled with illumination for those who are open to receive. The flight of the eagle brings the energy of the mountain peaks, the places of vision and perception, to the world below.

Air represents the beginning of individuated life. With the first breath, the child enters his or her independent, physical existence. Thus, pulling the Air card can indicate a new beginning, a new phase of life.

Air is a mental element and suggests intellectual activity. It is an element of inspiration and poetic creativity. When thoughts are flowing creatively, there is a feeling of spaciousness in the awareness. When thoughts are heavy and stuck in a pattern that is not serving, there is a feeling of constriction and claustrophobia. If your mind is filled with conflicting thoughts, the Air element can bring clarity.

The element Air is a force that can both direct and open your path. Air can focus energy or disperse it. Its effect depends upon your intention. Intention is like a flute, an instrument through which the air is channeled. When we construct our instrument with care, we are able to direct our course more effectively.

If you would like to increase your rapport with the Air element, find a place outdoors where you can stand quietly and allow the air to move through your whole body, lifting the tensions and confusions from your mind and carrying them away as the wind carries leaves that are no longer needed.

"Supple like a tree in the wind,
he has no destination in view
and makes use of anything
life happens to bring his way."
Tao Te Ching[4]

FIRE

Solar energy. Life.
Creativity. Transformation. Catalyst.
Sexuality. Luminosity. Transference of power from one form to another.
Beauty. Illumination. Passion.

"I am that supreme and fiery force that sends forth all the sparks of life. . . . I am that living and fiery essence of the divine substance that flows in the beauty of the fields. I shine in the water, I burn in the sun and the moon and the stars. . . . I am life."

—Hildegarde of Bingen[5]

Fire exists deep in the Earth—a force that has powered the creation of the material world, of planet Earth herself. Fire also exists outside the Earth in the Sun. An active sun burns inside the core of the Earth, and an active Sun burns at the center of our solar system—fire within and fire without. Just as the Sun is called a "star" by astronomers, so is there a star inside the Earth; and just as there is a fiery star inside the Earth, so there is a fiery star inside each one of us.

When you pull the Fire card, you are being encouraged to connect with the fiery star inside you—to make use of your own solar energy. With solar energy, we express our passion, our creativity, and our insight. This energy is expressed through sexuality, through dance, through music, through the arts, and through every activity, no matter how apparently mundane, that is engaged in with passion.

We all know that fire burns, and inherent in the Fire card is a caution to be respectful of the power of the fire. At times, burning is necessary. Forests periodically catch fire, and, over time, through this apparent destruction, they transform into new, vital, and healthy growth. If you are enduring a time of fiery destruction, know that the old forms need to be destroyed in order to make space for the new life.

Fire is the energy of the inner star, of the heart, and of relationship and friendship. For millennia, we have gathered around the fire—to keep warm, to stay safe from predators, and to tell stories filled with spiritual essence. Fire reminds us to invite and provide companionship, to share, and to protect.

"We all cook together around a fire
Our yearning music builds.

We share our tools and instruments and plates;
We are companions on this earth

As the sun and planets are in the sky.
We are all sentries at our sacred humble posts."

—Hafiz[6]

WATER

Fecund. Embodying the potential of all material forms. Womb. Ripe. Mother Ocean. Depths that are unfathomable. Cleansing. Healing. Refreshing. Relieves emotions. Variability within a universal rhythm.

"Understanding the fact that we are essentially water is the key to uncovering the mysteries of the universe. If you reexamine the world around you from this new perspective, you will start to see things as you have never seen them before."

—**Masaru Emoto**[7]

Water absorbs the primordial Radiance from Air and Sun and releases that Radiance into the Earth. Water is the source of our physical lives. Water is potentiality—the fluid yet material manifestation of the energy that was transferred from the Radiance by the Air.

When you pull the Water card, you are being reminded of your potential to flow in any direction. Water reminds us that we are not static beings with a single form or a single capacity. We are like a river that is constantly transforming. The Water card asks you to flow with the current of your life, to not set up barriers in the mind.

Water is the element of wonder and surprise. Pulling this card may indicate an unexpected person or event is or will be entering your life. You are being counseled to experience this unexpected person or event without preconceived ideas and limitations.

Water also speaks to the emotions and counsels trust in the sometimes incomprehensible (to the mind) power of our emotional nature. Our emotions are clues to the deep ocean that we all inhabit and that connects us with the Radiance. If you have pulled the Water card, take time to be with your emotions in solitude. Do not ignore, repress, or project your emotions. Be quiet. Feel the emotions and allow them to flow through you. Pulling the Water card reminds you to respect your emotions but not to be ruled by them.

The Water card also counsels you to use the element of water consciously in your life, knowing that it is an ally that can help you cleanse and renew. This may take any form of practice that appeals to you—walking by the river, swimming, floating on the lake, drinking more water, taking more baths. It may mean taking part in water restoration activities in your geographic area.

"Nothing in the world
is as soft and yielding as water.
Yet for dissolving the hard and inflexible,
nothing can surpass it."
Tao Te Ching[8]

EARTH

Foundation. Stability. Trust.
Green. Lively. Nourishment. Mother.
Plants, animals, birds, sea creatures, insects, bacteria, viruses, molds—all life forms.
Rocks. Minerals. Forests. Mountains.

"Mountains have long been a geography for pilgrimage, places where peoples have been humbled and strengthened. They are symbols of the Sacred Center. Many have traveled to them in order to find the concentrated energy of Earth and to realize the strength of unimpeded space."

—**Joan Halifax**[9]

Earth is the firm foundation beneath our feet. It is the concrete, physical result of the actions of Radiance permeating Air, Fire, and Water. Earth is this life and this world.

With Air, Water, and Fire, Earth creates our home—the place where our physical bodies reside. Through photosynthesis of solar energy, the plants of Earth feed us. Earth is our mother. She nourishes us both with food grown from her soil and with the concrete manifestation of the Radiance in her many forms—roses, butterflies, hummingbirds—every life form that feeds and nourishes us with beauty. This element is reflected in our bones and flesh.

When you pull the Earth card, you are being counseled to reflect on the ways you nourish yourself and to correct any imbalances that may exist in your diet, exercise, or contact with nature. These three areas—food, movement, and time spent in nature—are ways we replenish and substantiate the Earth element in ourselves.

Take time to encounter the Earth element each day, preparing your food with care and with gratitude, taking time to care for animals or a garden. Engaging in a nurturing way with the Earth is nurturing to the caregiver. Remember that your body is also the earth. Exercise and dance will strengthen the earth element in your body.

It is most important to approach the manifestations of the Earth element with respect and gratitude. Our physical lives are dependent upon the health and wellbeing of Mother Earth. The care we give to the Earth is the care we give to ourselves.

> ". . . the human, in making contact with the sacred through plants, must go into the world of plants, not as a human who knows everything, but as a seeker who has come to learn."
>
> —**Stephen Buhner**[10]

CHILD

SEED. ENCAPSULATED. PROTECTED. INNOCENT. FRESH. HAPPINESS. PLAYFULNESS. VULNERABILITY. THE GREAT AWAKENER. CODE. ORIGINAL NATURE.

"There was a child went forth every day,
And the first object he look'd upon, that object he became,
And that object became part of him for
the day or a certain part of the day,
Or for many years or stretching cycles of years.

The early lilacs became part of this child,
And grass and white and red morning-glories,
and white and red clover,
And the song of the phoebe-bird."

—**Walt Whitman**[11]

We all begin human life as the Child—a being of miraculous origin with untold potential. The Child is the "great awakener," a seemingly helpless newborn whose entrance into the world sends unforeseen ripples of opportunity, challenge, and complexity through the lives of his or her family and community.

The Child lives on in all of us throughout our entire lives. The seed that we are when we are born is replicated in the DNA of every cell. This fundamental miracle of all life is often disregarded because it is so common. Yet when reflected upon, its miraculous nature is apparent. Every cell of the body carries a code that refers not only to that cell but also to the whole organism of which it is a part.

When you pull the Child card, you are being counseled to reach deep inside yourself to the "original code"—your own seeded nature—to access your personal, primary nature—your true self.

The Child in each of us wants to play and recognizes the value of play, for it is in play that we access the seed. Remember to include time every day for true play. Play is often the way we encounter our original code. What we enjoy without ponderous thought is a key to our "original nature."

The Child card speaks of your innocence and your vulnerability but also speaks of protection, reminding you that, as with the DNA in each of your cells, there is a universal code of which we are all a part and through which each of us is included, tutored, and received.

> "Many indigenous societies believe that we all possess 'original medicine:' personal power, duplicated nowhere else on the planet. No two individuals carry the same combination of talents or challenges."
>
> —**Angeles Arrien**[12]

NEST

One's home, family, community.
Feeling "at home," comfortable, safe.
Retreat. Security. "Sleepy Land."

"God bless the house,
From site to stay,
From beam to wall
From end to end,
From ridge to basement,
From balk to roof-tree,
From found to summit,
Found and summit."
—**Alexander Carmichael**[13]

Our Nest is the safe place represented by home, family, and community in their archetypal aspects. Even if one does not actually feel safe in one's home, family, or community, there is still an archetypal force of safety that is represented in the Nest card.

This archetypal safety zone is the place we retreat to, either literally or figuratively, when we feel threatened or when we need time to restore our vital forces. It may or may not be a geographic location. It could be a place within the psyche.

The value of the nest cannot be overestimated. All beings need a safety-zone where they are nurtured and supported and taught basic skills that help them fly. Often there are parents or other important elders who participate in the nesting phase.

Pulling the Nest card suggests that either you are now in a "safety zone," or you need to find one. Nest invites you to retreat for a time, to pull back, to stay quiet, and look about you. In addition, the nest card suggests that you may need to seek counsel and support from elders you trust. These elders may be family members, friends, teachers, spiritual counselors, or other human guides. They may be people you have yet to meet and need to find. Or, you may find your guides in nature, in the wind, in the sunlight, in waterfalls or lakes, or in the plants and animals. Guides come in many guises.

It is important to honor the need for a nesting phase, to trust its value, and to allow yourself to experience nurturing, safety, and wisdom. However, there is also a danger of falling asleep in one's nest for far too long. This is the state that Joseph Campbell called "sleepy land." Fortunately, Life is very wise. When we have stayed in the nest too long, when we have fallen asleep to our own growth, Life has many ways of calling us to awaken.

You will know that it is time to leave your nest when you become uncomfortable, dissatisfied, bored, worried, etc. Often, leaving the nest does not mean a literal move from one residence to another, but rather an inner move—a change in our way of perceiving and feeling. This may be letting go of beliefs or inner patterns that no longer serve.

"The hero's journey must begin with the call.
One way or another, a guide must come to say, 'Look,
you're in Sleepy Land. Wake. Come on a trip. There is a
whole aspect of your consciousness, your being, that's
not been touched. So you're at home here? Well,
there's not enough of you there.' And so it starts."

—**Joseph Campbell**[14]

HERO/ HEROINE

LEAVING THE NEST. MOVING FORWARD IN LIFE. INDIVIDUATION. MASCULINE AND FEMININE ENERGIES. COURAGE. STRENGTH. FORTITUDE. YIN/YANG.

"The goal of the hero trip
down to the jewel point
is to find those levels in the psyche
that open, open, open,
and finally open to the mystery
of your Self being
Buddha consciousness
Or the Christ.

That's the journey.
It is all about finding
that still point in your mind."

—**Joseph Campbell**[15]

The Hero/Heroine card symbolizes the positive energy of the courageous person who enters the journey of life willing to take on the challenges that come his or her way. The Hero/Heroine must leave the familiar and the known. He or she is genuinely courageous—a characteristic that is not always recognized by others. True courage is not bravado. It is the ability to admit that one is frightened and to take measured and wise steps forward in spite of the fear.

You are being reminded as well to see your fears for what they are. Ignoring fear can lead us into danger. Dwelling in fear can cause us to exaggerate the dangers. A reasonable assessment of danger is a trait of the Hero/Heroine.

This card also symbolizes the power that comes when masculine and feminine energies are combined and harmonized. When you pull the Hero/Heroine card, you are being guided to call on both your masculine and feminine qualities—the yin and yang aspects of your nature—to assist you in your life journey. You are being reminded that you need both the capacity to advance (yang) and the capacity to listen and be receptive (yin) if you are to successfully embody the energy of the Hero/Heroine.

"There is no greater illusion than fear,
no greater wrong than preparing to defend yourself,
no greater misfortune than having an enemy.

Whoever can see through all fear
will always be safe."

Tao Te Ching[16]

TRAVEL

The "Way." The journey of life.
The Tao. The Call. Beckoning.
Opportunity. Exploration. The Unknown.
New Horizons. Adventure. Leaving
the community. Foreign Lands.

"People have traveled over this earth with a heart of inquiry for millennia. They have sung through the land as a living being, offered themselves, their steps, their voices and prayers as acts of purification that opened them to an experience of connectedness."

—Joan Halifax[17]

Travel is the journey of life, the Way, the Tao. When you pull the Travel card, you may be about to begin a new cycle in your life. The card may indicate a child about to be born, a new job, or a new geographic location. It may indicate meeting someone new or the loss of a loved person, animal companion, or beloved home in preparation for a journey to a new place or condition.

The Travel card may indicate, simply, that you are about to take a trip—either short or long distance—perhaps to visit a long-time friend or family members, or to visit the land of your ancestors. It may also indicate a journey to a country you have never visited or the learning of a new language or skill.

The Travel card may also indicate travel on the inner planes. At this time in your life, you may be traveling spiritually. Your interest in esoteric and spiritual matters may be deepening. A new interest in spirituality, Western or Eastern religions, transcendentalism, theosophy, spiritualism, anthroposophy, or astrology may be growing in you. You may be having extraordinary dreams or daytime, waking visions.

You may be especially interested in music, nature, and/or the arts at this time. In whatever way you are experiencing Travel, typically when one pulls this card, it means that you are hearing the "call" to become more than you have been, to let go of the holds that bind, and to embrace the adventure of moving outside the comfort and familiarity of home.

"As you go the way of life,
you will see a great chasm.
Jump.
It is not as wide as you think."
—**Joseph Campbell**[18]

WILLINGNESS

POSITIVE CHOICE. NOW. PRESENT MOMENT AWARENESS. WILLPOWER. DETERMINATION. TRUST. READINESS.

"The warrior's approach
is to say 'yes' to life:
'yea' to it all."
—**Joseph Campbell**[19]

Willingness is the energy of assent. It is saying "yes" to life even when we are afraid. Willingness is not forcing oneself, however. It is a genuinely positive attitude toward life and its challenges.

When you pull the Willingness card, you are being encouraged to ask yourself if the blocks and obstacles that you are experiencing in your life are due to outside forces or to inner ambivalence. Often, the mind or personality will say, "Yes. I am willing," but at a deeper level, a fundamental aspect of our being is saying, "No."

It can be very difficult to get in touch with the part of us that is saying, "No," but once we recognize that outer limits may be connected to an inner limit, we can pause and reflect, asking the question, "What part of me is it that is not willing?"

It is important to recognize that the part of us that is not willing carries its own wisdom. We need not conclude that in order to move forward in life, we must find a way to transform our unwillingness into willingness. Often, we are ambivalent for a good reason. Perhaps our mind has set goals for us that we believe will further our growth, but at a deeper level we sense that those goals are not in our best interest. There are many reasons for ambivalence, and we must be careful and respectful of ourselves when we feel reluctance.

The Willingness card reminds us to respect "right-timing." When it is time to go forward, uncovering our ambivalence will feel like a fresh breeze moving through the open windows of our house. Simply realizing that we have been unwilling will clear the mind, and we will feel ready and able to say, "Yes."

"There is a time for being ahead,
A time for being behind;
A time for being in motion,
A time for being at rest;
A time for being vigorous,
A time for being exhausted;
A time for being safe,
A time for being in danger."

Tao Te Ching[20]

FORCE/ EGO

THE EGO. THE PERSONALITY IN THIS LIFETIME. A PARTIAL VIEW. THE TENDENCY TO PUSH TO GET ONE'S WAY.

"People try to force issues only when not realizing that it can't be done—that there is no way of deviating from the watercourse of nature. You may imagine that you are outside, or separate from, the Tao and thus able to follow it or not follow; but this very imagination is itself within the stream for there is no way other than the Way."

—**Alan Watts**[21]

Force/Ego represents the human personality with its fears and desires and conscious and unconscious attitudes and habits. When the personality's wants and fears dominate without adequate reflection and self-awareness, the tendency is to use force to get one's way.

This use of force can be inner or outer directed—meaning that at times we apply this energy to force ourselves and at other times we use this energy to force others. In either case, the use of force does violence to our inner peace and personal growth and often does harm to others.

Drawing this card asks you to reflect on areas in your life where you force yourself or others. It is tempting to try to force one's way past obstacles, but this only works superficially and temporarily. Force/Ego must be transformed into an energy that serves the hero/heroine rather than undermines.

If one is caught in the habit of using force, this can be released through knowing that there is a proper time for all things and that it is never necessary to force. "Your own will come to you," say the wise.

Spending time in nature in close contact with the elements of Air, Fire, Water, and Earth can restore our balance and inner peace. When we feel connected to the natural flow of the world, we realize there is no need to push.

"Rushing into action, you fail.
Trying to grasp things, you lose them.
Forcing a project to completion,
you ruin what was almost ripe."
Tao Te Ching[22]

THRESHOLD/ GUARDIAN

Openings. Doorways. Arches. Challenges. Hoops. Gates. Rites of Passage. Blocks. Obstacles. Danger. Barrier. Monsters. Fears. Resistance. Guardians. Trickery. Breakthrough. Wisdom. Transformation. Magic.

"When you cross the threshold, you are passing into the dark forest, taking a plunge into the sea, embarking upon the night sea journey."
—**Joseph Campbell**[23]

"When we pass through this door, we always lose something. Something must be sacrificed."
—**Joan Halifax**[24]

On every life journey, we cross many thresholds. The Threshold/ Guardian card speaks of the many encounters we have in our lives as we are moving from one phase, one way of being, to another.

Being born is a threshold; entering school is a threshold; puberty is a threshold; graduation, marriage, giving birth, divorce, starting a job, leaving a job, moving to a new geographical location, illness, death—all are thresholds.

Some thresholds feel like burdens or obstacles. We know that we want to travel from the place we are in now to the next place, but we cannot get there and feel frustrated and blocked either for known or unknown reasons—often both.

When you pull the Threshold/Guardian card, you are standing before an archway—a transition zone between the life you are living now and the life you will be living once you have passed through the arch. As Joseph Campbell demonstrated, in the myths of many cultures, the threshold is a common motif. Central to the experience of the threshold is the gate—the structure that bars the way, that says, "Beware." Often, there is a guardian at this gate—one who warns, or prevents, or distracts from forward movement.

When you pull the Threshold/Guardian card, you are being asked, first, to see that you are standing at the end of one phase and on the brink of a new one. Additionally, you are being asked to recognize the guardian at the gate. The guardian represents the fears and/or desires that hold you in the phase of life in which you are standing now. In order to unlock the gate and pass through, you must see what is blocking you and transform the energy into an energy that assists you.

Sometimes, it is a gift that transforms the guardian; sometimes a sacrifice. Sometimes the hero or heroine must outwit the guardian through trickery or magic. When you pull the Threshold/Guardian card, know that you have your own bag of tricks—your wisdom, your strength, your wit, and your skills—upon which you can rely to appease the guardian, unlock the gate, and pass through.

> "Here again we have . . . a symbol of great antiquity, the bridge as threshold—that which at the same time separates and conjoins two worlds, a reconciler of opposites. The bridge, too, outwits the devil—who is known to abhor whatever unites, and whose arch-enemy is running water—by providing a means for the soul's crossing from one stage to another."
>
> —**P. L. Travers**[25]

SEDUCTION

Enchantment. Siren song. Dreamland.
Neptune. Mystery. Mists. Veiled.
Confusion. Illusion. Deception. Ghosts.

"Morning and evening
Maids heard the goblins cry:
Come buy our orchard fruits,
Come buy, come buy: . . .
Our grapes fresh from the vine,
Pomegranates full and fine,
. . . Sweet to tongue and sound to eye;
Come buy, come buy."
—**Christina Rossetti**[26]

Once the hero or heroine has succeeded in appeasing the guardian and crossing the threshold into the new life, the challenges of the journey intensify. With each gate we unlock, with each threshold we cross, we accumulate strength, power, and wisdom. But lest we become complacent and assume we have now succeeded, Life continues to confront us with challenges and opportunities to grow.

Seduction is an experience that can happen at any phase of our life journey. With seduction, something apparently lovely is offered in exchange for which the hero or heroine must give up something he or she values. Often what must be given up is one's independence and adulthood. Through listening to the call, being willing, and then crossing the threshold, one has succeeded in becoming the authority for one's own life only to encounter a seduction that threatens that autonomy.

When you pull the Seduction card, you are being asked to recognize where you may be deceiving yourself by pretending that something lifeless is vital. In the fairy tale, Snow White is offered a beautiful apple. It seems to have life, but actually it is poisoned and carries death.

When what we thought was beautiful and life-giving reveals itself as rotten and death-dealing, we become disillusioned. Our heart is broken. The revelation of deception—which often is our own mind and personality refusing to see something—can cause us to feel that all of life has lost its meaning and value.

If you are experiencing this degree of loss and sorrow, take heart. Remember that when Snow White takes a bite of the apple, she first falls into the abyss of seeming-death. But just as the apple is not only an apple, Snow White's death is not only death. It is the beginning of a new life brought about by rejoining with a part of herself—the Prince (her yang side) that she had abandoned. The kiss of the Prince awakens Snow White to the new life by reminding her of the aspect of herself that she had cut off—her autonomy, integrity, and personal authority. When you have pulled the Seduction card, ask yourself, "Where is Life offering me the kiss of new life?"

"God has given us, in a measure, the power to make our own fate; when our energies seem to demand a sustenance they cannot get—when our will strains after a path we may not follow—we need neither starve from inanition, nor stand still in despair: we have but to seek another nourishment for the mind, as strong as the forbidden food it longed to taste—and perhaps surer."

—Charlotte Bronte[27]

BETRAYAL/ CHASM

FEAR. MISPERCEPTION. ILLUSION. TREACHERY. DANGER. A LEAP OF FAITH

"Betrayal. A wounding of the soul that acts as an agent of the sacred, marking an end of unconscious trust and providing impetus for growth."

—Jean Houston[28]

Betrayal/Chasm is the experience of fear and darkness—sometimes in the mind only and not in our actual circumstances. When we are in this energy, we cannot see clearly. We feel, as in Dante, that we have entered "a dark wood where the right path is wholly lost and gone."[29]

Betrayal/Chasm is the dark night of the soul, the "night sea journey."[30] We feel that before us yawns a chasm impossibly wide and behind us a wall prevents retreat. Though we know that the only way to move is to go forward, we are certain that we do not have the strength or the skill necessary to jump across the wide chasm that opens between us and the as-yet-veiled life on the other side.

When you pull the Betrayal/Chasm card, you may be in a situation that seems to be beyond your capacity or you may be experiencing fears that are unfounded in reality. If you are in the first condition, remember that the Radiance exists in all things. Even when we are in the midst of trouble, wisdom, light, and strength are available to us. It is often in the most difficult situations that we discover inner reserves of faith and strength that we did not know we possessed.

More often, one pulls this card when the fears in one's mind make it seem that a situation is beyond our capacity. Typically, these fears come from ancient wounding. To overcome these fears, it is important to enter into the healing power of Nature, taking time to sit by a river, to walk in the woods, to camp in the mountains. Time in nature will quiet the mind and allow the healing wisdom of the Radiance to speak.

"It is by going down into the abyss
that we recover the treasures of life.

Where you stumble,
there lies your treasure.

The very cave you are afraid to enter
turns out to be the source of
what you are looking for."

—Joseph Campbell[31]

TEARS/ GRIEVING

SADNESS. LOSS. FEAR OF LOSS. ANTICIPATING TROUBLE. CLEANSING. THE TRANSFORMATIVE POWER OF WATER. A NECESSARY EXPRESSION OF EMOTION. RESTORATION. BAPTISM.

"This brings us to the final formula of the Bodhisattava way, the way of the one who is grounded in eternity and moving in the field of time. The field of time is the field of sorrow. 'All life is sorrowful.' And it is. If you try to correct the sorrows, all you do is shift them somewhere else. Life is sorrowful. How do you live with that?"
—**Joseph Campbell**[32]

Tears/Grieving represents the necessary outpouring of emotions of loss and sadness. When we cry, we are cleansing ourselves, releasing toxins, and preparing ourselves for a new life. Crying is a form of cleansing, a way of washing away what is no longer needed—the thoughts and emotions that are keeping us caught in the past. When we cry fully without restraint, we begin a process of restoration.

When you pull the Tears/Grieving card, know that it is okay and reasonable to feel sadness at this time in your life. Allow the sadness to be expressed. Sometimes the companionship of a silent witness—a friend, animal companion, a flower, the presence of the elements—can help the tears flow and can help the cleansing process be complete.

If you are carrying long-held sadness, it is very important that you put the burden down. A ceremony is a powerful way of allowing old tears and sadness to be released. You can use any one of the elements, or all of them, for the process: washing away the burden with water; allowing sadness to blow away in the wind; putting your sorrow in the fire; or returning it to earth—any or all of these simple ceremonies will bring great healing.

When you pull the Tears/Grieving card, it is important to remember that feeling and expressing sadness are not the same as dwelling and living in sadness. The first is healing; the latter is disabling. Sadness is a natural part of human life and is not to be feared or suppressed, but be careful that you do not cling to your sadness. Feel it and then move on.

"You realize the eternal within yourself. You disengage, and yet, reengage. You—and here's the beautiful formula—'participate with joy in the sorrows of the world.' You play the game. It hurts, but you know that you have found the place that is transcendent of injury and fulfillments."

—**Joseph Campbell**[33]

THE JUDGE

Inner critic. "Group-speak." Finding fault. Restriction coming from inside or outside or both. Also: Careful thought. Precision. Discrimination. Wise perception.

"Sometimes you continue with old paths, even when your heart tells you not to. You may be staying on a path because it is the only one you know. Out of fear, you dare not think of yourself as anything but a daughter, son, partner, father, mother, executive, housewife, or student. Fears of new roles, financial insecurity, and even closed-mindedness to new experiences keep you from significantly changing and living your dreamingbody in the world. You feel obliged both to yourself and to others to maintain the personal history that you have created. Personal history is a prison that you seem to have created for yourself."

—**Arnie Mindell**[34]

The Judge card represents both the voices that criticize and belittle, waylaying us on our path, and the voices that help us through careful and precise thinking and discrimination. When you pull The Judge card, you are being asked to reflect on the voices speaking inside and outside you. Notice in yourself the energy of devaluing your worth, or the energy of recognizing your power. Do you speak your truth with discrimination?

The inner critic does not permit experimentation or invention, but wants life to proceed along habitual, clearly marked paths. The discriminator, on the other hand, is capable of balancing value and risk and choosing a way that is nourishing and growth-promoting, even if risky.

The Judge card reminds us that the capacity to be self-reflective and to observe oneself with curiosity in order to learn and grow is an important attribute of maturity. A positive use of The Judge energy is necessary to human survival.

The Judge can be a useful ally if we utilize the skill of discernment. The challenge is to transform the inner critic from one who clouds awareness with self-doubt to one who assists awareness through processes of awakening—coming to adulthood and self-determination.

"For beginners, I recommend the method of pure recognition: recognition without judgment. Feelings, whether of compassion or irritation, should be welcomed, recognized, and treated on an absolutely equal basis: because both are ourselves."

—**Thich Nhat Hanh**[35]

CROSSROADS

MOVEMENT. CHOICES. NEW VISTAS. ALLIES. DECISION. MANY PATHS. DIVERGENCE. CONVERGENCE. MEETINGS. CENTER. DESTINY. RECOGNITION.

"You road I enter upon and look around,
I believe you are not all that is here,
I believe that much unseen is also here."
—**Walt Whitman**[36]

The Crossroads card is the card of many paths diverging and converging. It is the center of the wheel where the revolving spokes join. At the crossroads, we encounter our destiny—but the destiny is written by the choices we make there.

There is often unseen energy at the crossroads. This truth is figured mythically in the Greek story of Oedipus. At the crossroads, Oedipus meets an old man who is blocking his way. In fury, Oedipus kills the old man. Later, he learns that the old man was his father. One of the many messages of this myth is, "Stand still and develop the power of genuine sight when you are at a crossroads." At the crossroads, we must understand the energy we encounter before proceeding. If we act in haste, we may destroy something of value without knowing what we have destroyed. Thus, recognition is necessary before we can move forward.

When you pull the Crossroads card, you may be at a time in your life when you need to make a choice between options that seem equally fair or, conversely, equally bleak. Central to choosing is the process of utilizing both heart and mind in making the choice.

If you have pulled the Crossroads card, you are being counseled to listen deeply before making your choice. Spending time in solitude in a natural setting makes it easier to hear the song in your heart and the wisdom in your mind. At the Crossroads, precipitous action results in imbalance. Wait quietly for the right choice to make itself known.

"Do you have the patience to wait
Until your mud settles,
And the right action arises by itself?"
Tao Te Ching[37]

SILENCE

Pausing. Resting. Becoming quiet.
Inner peace. Inner light. Solitude.
Spaciousness. Open access to Divine wisdom.

"Silence is where we learn to listen, where we learn to see. Holding silence, being held by stillness, Buddhists and tribal people go alone to the wilderness 'to stop and see,' to renew their vision, to enter the mind ground, to hear the truth, to return to the knowledge of self and the truth of no self."

—**Joan Halifax**[38]

Silence is a state we carry with us at all times, even though the busy desire-driven or fear-driven chatter of the mind often entirely obscures it. Silence is here, in this moment, now.

The great benefit of Silence is that when the mind becomes quiet, insights begin to take the place of the chatter. Inner peacefulness and restfulness are felt. No longer is one hurrying because of fear or desire; no longer is one trying to escape the past or avoid the future or, conversely, wishing for the past to return or for the future to arrive now. In silence, we feel our blessed eternal state—the present moment.

When you draw the Silence card, you are being encouraged to dwell in the present moment. The oracle is reminding you that all problems have a solution. In their own way and in their own time, all things arrive. There is no need to fear, to strive, to push, to pull. Rest. Reflect. Be silent. Allow your own wisdom to be your guide.

"The wicasa wakan loves the silence, wrapping it around himself like a blanket—a loud silence with a voice like thunder which tells him of many things."
—Lakota John Fire Lame Deer[39]

OLD KNOWLEDGE

FAMILY LORE. COMMUNITY WISDOM. ORAL AND WRITTEN TRADITIONS. BARDS. MONKS. SCRIBES. ILLUMINATED MANUSCRIPTS. ANCIENT RECORDS. RUNES. INSCRIPTIONS. LOST LANGUAGES.

"Ask the wild bee what the Druids knew." Old English Adage

—P. L. Travers[40]

Old Knowledge refers to ancient wisdom that has been passed on through many generations through oral or written traditions. It is the collective wisdom of the species that sometimes lies abandoned and forgotten. In ancient times, recording and transmitting knowledge was a sacred responsibility, saving mystical information for future generations.

When you pull Old Knowledge, you are being counseled to do research into ancient traditions as a way of deepening your own wisdom. You are being encouraged to let go of "group-think," usually represented in the mass media and often embedded in attitudes of academe, and to find the wisdom of the root people.

This wisdom may be written down in ancient illuminated manuscripts, in forgotten languages, in runes or inscriptions, in rock paintings, and/or this wisdom may be retained in the oral traditions of grandmothers' stories or in the simple, daily activities of people who still live close to the Earth.

When you pull Old Knowledge, seek the wisdom of your parents, grandparents, and ancestors. Visiting the root people, indigenous elders who have access to the wisdom of their people, can be very helpful.

"Story telling is the most ancient form of education. It is about the remembering, making, and sharing of images that bind together time, nature, and a people. Stories, like the sacred plants, are medicine and food come from the Earth. They remind us that we do not stand alone. Through them we live in the body of coyote and crow, tree and stone, gods and heroes, Ancestral Mothers and Grandmothers."

—Joan Halifax[41]

THE INNER DOOR

BECOMING AN "INITIATE." SEEKING. FINDING. ENTERING MYSTICAL UNION. SPIRITUAL INSIGHT.

"Ask and it shall be given you; seek and you shall find; knock and it shall be opened unto you. For every one that asketh receiveth; and he that seeketh findeth; and to him that knocketh it shall be opened."

Bible, Matthew 7:7-8, 42

The Inner Door is the path of the person who cares more for genuine wisdom than for the things of this world, one who recognizes that his or her origins come from afar.

This card is an affirmation. It tells you that you have arrived, that you have successfully crossed from the mundane world of illusion into the higher world of wisdom. You are now an "Initiate."

The Initiate does not identify with the physical body, with the emotions, or with the mind as the center of being. Rather, the

Initiate knows that the body, emotions, and thoughts are transitory like ripples on the surface of a pond. The initiate seeks to experience the Radiance in all things, in all events, in all moments and gives thanks in every time and in every place.

> "I did not at once meet with the M., but first somcone sent by him who was completely initiated into the mysteries of the effects of all plants and their connection with the universe and with man's nature."
>
> —**Rudolf Steiner**[43]

LETTING GO

TRUST. RELEASE. FEELINGS OF RELIEF.
THE OPEN HAND. FLOATING ON
THE RIVER OF LIFE. FREEDOM. JOYFULNESS.

"True mastery can be gained
by letting things go their own way.
It can't be gained by interfering."
Tao Te Ching[44]

Letting go refers to those times when we live life openly and with trust. When we let go, we surrender ourselves to the flow of the river and stop resisting the current of our lives. Often tears precede letting go and faith follows from letting go.

If you have pulled the Letting Go card, you are being encouraged to clean house—both literally and figuratively. What have you stored in old shoeboxes in the closet? What have you stored in the basement? In the attic? These locations are the places where we weigh ourselves down with material and/or psychological clutter and baggage that is making it difficult for us to move forward in life.

Cleaning house is a powerful ceremony for someone who wants to let go more in life. Similarly, gliding down a river in a canoe or floating lazily on a beautiful lake are actual practices that we can do to help us learn how to let go.

If you are carrying many burdens either material or psychological, reflect on the message of scripture that tells us how difficult it is for a rich man to enter heaven. This is not because he lacks moral character. It is simply because material wealth can trick us into becoming so attached to the things of this world that we lose awareness of our essential Radiance. That essential Radiance does not exist in that shoe box in the attic. It came with us when we were born naked with no possessions, and it is with us when we leave this life, having to forfeit even our physical bodies.

Simple, regular practice of house cleaning—of giving things away—especially things we value—prepares us for the ultimate letting go when we leave our physical bodies.

We are not our bodies. We are the Radiance. The Radiance has no trouble flowing through the eye of the needle.

"The Tao never does anything,
yet through it, all things are done."
Tao Te Ching[45]

FAITH

UNSHAKEABLE KNOWLEDGE THAT COMES FROM DEEP WITHIN. INTUITION. GRACE. SPIRITUAL ENLIGHTENMENT. TRUST. SECURITY.

"Our dead never forget this beautiful world that gave them being. They still love its verdant valleys, its murmuring rivers, its magnificent mountains, sequestered vales and verdant lined lakes and bays, and ever yearn in tender fond affection over the lonely hearted living, and often return to visit, guide, console, and comfort them."

—**Chief Seattle**[46]

Faith is an experience. It is not a theory, an idea, or a belief. It is knowing—deep, unquestioning knowing.

Your life is an unfolding path, a path that opens as you walk. Sometimes it is dark and the path is not visible, but still the path is there. If you are frightened, sit quietly in nature and you will again be able to feel the path beneath your feet.

Thoughts in the mind and emotions like fear and desire interfere with our capacity to feel our connection to the Source of our being, but not being able to feel the Source does not mean that it is not there.

When you pull the Faith card, you are being guided to place your trust in the Radiance that exists in all things, that is with you in every moment and in every place. Faith does not come through effort, it comes through quiet. Faith does not need to be acquired or gained; it already exists within you.

"This way is opposed to all human reason . . .
you can advance on this path only by faith, not by sight . . .
Do not be anxious about tomorrow. . . . Whether you be
waking or sleeping, by night and by day, the seed
sprouts and grows, you know not how."

—**The Rule of Taize**[47]

FOCUS

"Thought is a living force."

THE CREATIVE POWER OF THOUGHTS. INTENTION. PREPARATION. GATHERING ONE'S FORCES. MANIFESTING THE DREAM.

". . . as I tell the story it will begin to happen."
— **Leslie Marmon Silko**[48]

The Focus card includes a quotation from Rudolf Steiner: "Thought is a living force."[49] Thoughts literally create our reality. The force of our thoughts has the power to influence material reality in the same way that a bowling ball rolling down an alley has the power to tumble the nine pins. Thought is the bowling ball. Material reality is the nine pins.

When you pull this card, you are being asked to carefully and honestly examine your own thoughts. What are you creating every day? Notice in any given moment where you place your attention.

Attention is energy. If we keep having the same thoughts, we are giving energy to those thoughts and are more likely to see the world through the lens of those thoughts and also to create circumstances in our lives that stem from those thoughts.

Sitting meditation can be an excellent practice for training the attention. Through sitting meditation, we develop more control over our thought process. We learn to withdraw energy from unproductive thought patterns and to give energy to positive, creative thought forms. We develop the ability to choose where we put our attention in any given moment. We can then focus our thought force more and more effectively to produce inner harmony and outer beauty.

"The aspirant can perform no greater service for his world than to be mindful that his acts, even his thoughts and speech, become part of the condition of the world."

—**Doug Boyd**[50]

GRATITUDE

EXPRESSIONS OF THANKSGIVING.
A WARM HEART. INNER THANKFULNESS.
ACCEPTANCE. ALIGNMENT WITH WHAT IS.

"O happy living things! No tongue
Their beauty might declare:
A spring of love gush'd from my heart,
And I bless'd them unaware:
Sure my kind saint took pity on me,
And I bless'd them unaware.

The selfsame moment I could pray;
And from my neck so free
The Albatross fell off, and sank
Like lead into the sea."

—Samuel Taylor Coleridge[51]

Gratitude is the Way. It is the path. All the stepping stones are stones in which gratitude can be felt or claimed. Gratitude is the most profound key—unlocking every door. When we express our thankfulness in every place and in every moment, we are in a bliss state.

When you pull the Gratitude card, it is a reminder of all the beauty in your life. You are being counseled to look about you and see the beauty and to take concrete, ceremonial actions to demonstrate and experience your gratitude. Waking in the morning and bowing to the day is a way of expressing gratitude. Preparing a meal with awareness is a way of expressing gratitude. Taking a bath and feeling the soothing water is a way of expressing gratitude.

Especially transformational is the practice of giving thanks for the difficulties—all the blocks and obstacles—we experience in life. We are accustomed to giving thanks for experiences we like, but we often forget to give thanks for the experiences we do not like. Yet these difficulties are often our greatest teachers.

> "Such respect is not a feeling or an attitude only. It's a way of life. Such respect means that we never stop realizing and never neglect to carry out our obligation to ourselves and our environment."
>
> **—Doug Boyd**[52]

FORGIVENESS

A QUIET MIND. FEAR AND HATRED DISSOLVE.
ACCEPTANCE. SOFTNESS. BARRIERS DISSOLVE.

"He that is without sin among you,
let him first cast a stone at her."
Bible, John 8:7[53]

Forgiveness is a ceremony. When we feel injured by a person or by events, it is time for a ceremony. Forgiveness is not an intellectual activity; it is an experience—a spiritual practice based in the heart. Because forgiveness is so difficult for most people, it is helpful to enact the forgiveness ceremonially. This enactment may begin in the mind, but it is completed in the heart.

When you pull the Forgiveness card, take some time to be alone. Create a small, ceremonial space by laying a beautiful cloth on the ground or on a floor or table. On this cloth, place all four elements—a bowl of water, a flower or plant, a feather, and a lit candle. Also find an object—a shell, a stone, a piece of jewelry, etc.—that represents you, and find one or several objects that represent the person or persons or events that seem to have injured you.

Sit quietly in meditation until your thoughts have settled down. Then bring into your mind the Mayan chant, "En lak esh." "You are the other me." Repeat this chant to your inner child who is frightened and hurt. Pick up the object that represents you, and say, "You are the other me." Imagine that you are holding your inner child and comforting him or her. Then one by one, pick up the objects that represent the people or events that you feel have done you harm. Say in turn to each of them, "You are the other me." See the inner child—the vulnerability—in each person or event. Comfort each of them in turn.

At the end of the ceremony, say, "I forgive you" to yourself and to all those involved, including the events themselves.

Finally, give thanks for everything that has happened, remembering that the most difficult experiences also carry the Radiance.

"Knowing our wholeness directly in the meditation practice, we may find ourselves coming to terms with things as they are, a deepening of understanding and compassion, a lessening of anguish and despair."
—**Jon Kabat-Zinn**[54]

LOVE

An Open Heart. Warmth. Mothering. Fathering. Union. Light.

"Love is the threshold where divine and human presence ebb and flow into each other."
—John O'Donohue[55]

Love is the binding force of the Universe. It is the law of attraction between opposites—the negative pole of the magnet attracting the positive pole and vice versa. It is the binding together of atoms to create cells to create life. Being loving is planting a seed that in its own way and in its own time will grow and flourish.

When you pull the Love card, you are being reminded of this powerful, all-encompassing force. Love is the third that arises when two are joined. It is a newborn child, a flower, a bird flying. If you are in a time when you feel hurt, unloved, or abandoned, the Love card reminds you of the spiritual principle to "give that which you seek."

Love is not wanting; it is not something that can be demanded. In romantic relationships, we sometimes say, "I love you," when what we really mean is "I want you." "I want you" always involves, whether consciously or not, ideas and attitudes of ownership and obligation. "If you love me, you will ____." This is not love. This is possessiveness.

Genuine love is an act of giving. Rather than pulling energy toward us, we are emanating energy outwardly from our heart.

If you are having troubles in love, reflect upon the role you are playing in your relationships. Perhaps you are asking others to give to you and feeling cross when they don't. Allow yourself to trust the spiritual principle, "Your own will come to you." Those with whom we have a natural affinity appear in our lives if we are quiet, patient, and trusting of Spirit.

Simply be loving and, through the law of attraction, your love will return to you. Thus, the wise say, "When we want more love in our lives, we must give more love."

"Surrender yourself, give yourself, and good measure, pressed down, shaken together and running over will be poured into your lap. For the measure you give is the measure you will receive."

The Rule of Taize[56]

RECIPROCITY

GIVING AND RECEIVING. RECOGNITION OF BEAUTY. TAKING CARE OF THE WORLD.

". . . the Navajo would say . . . one needs to reestablish his relationship with the rhythms of nature. It is the ritual as well as the medicine which gets one back 'in shape.' The medicine may cure the symptoms, but it won't cure you. It does not put you back in step with . . . the natural cycles—this is a job for the 'singer.' . . . For many tribes . . . reciprocation is at the heart of everything going on in the world."

—Barre Toelken[57]

Reciprocity is one of the fundamental spiritual principles that helps us maintain balance in life. It is the spiritual recognition that, as the medicine man Rolling Thunder said, "Nothing comes free," and that in order to participate honorably in the creation, we must give back in full measure for what we have received.[59] The opposite of reciprocity is hoarding—the tense gathering up of goods, fearfully keeping them to ourselves. These "goods" can be material possessions or emotional ones. We might hoard our money, for example, or we might hoard our time, or our trust in another's capacities.

When we act reciprocally, we participate openly and freely in the dance of life, giving and receiving joy.

When you pull the Reciprocity card, you are being encouraged to notice the areas in your life where you give freely and receive freely as well as the areas where you are tense and find it difficult to receive or to give. The areas of tension and difficulty can gradually be healed by taking small steps to regularly say, "yes" gratefully when something is given to you and to notice where Life is asking you to give more.

Our sacred responsibility is to reciprocate for the Life given to us with expressions of respect, care, and gratitude.

"It was as though there was some law of invocation and response: one cannot be helped until he seeks help, cannot be taught until he tries to learn, cannot be answered unless he asks."

—**Doug Boyd**[58]

THE LOVER

THE BELOVED. AN IDEAL. SOUL MATE.
A PARTNER. COMPLETION. EMOTIONAL FULFILLMENT.
PLEASURE. RIPENESS. PURITY OF HEART.

"Beloved of the soul. One's double in the extended realm of the soul; . . . that one for whom one yearns, after whom one wanders, in search of potential reunion. For many people, the Beloved refers to the Divine Beloved within."

—**Jean Houston**[60]

The Lover card represents the pure heart, the heart of the child. The primordial Radiance glows through the eyes and the smile of the child and of the lover. The Lover card represents the ideal of the beloved—the one for whom we wait, the one we adore. The Lover energy is inside each one of us and at special times in our lives, it is evoked by the presence of another who embodies The Lover energy.

The Lover energy is not limited to human beings. We encounter this energy in everything that we experience as beautiful. As an ideal, The Lover represents the threshold to heaven, to paradise, to bliss, to complete trust and purity of heart.

When you pull The Lover card, you may have just met or you may be about to meet a special person—one who is or will become a romantic partner. Or you may have concerns about your current romantic relationship. Equally possible is that the ideal lover, the Beloved energy that you carry yourself, is now radiating more fully from you into the world. In this case, the card is telling you that you are The Lover. The card can also indicate that you are presently engaged in or about to become engaged in a life's work that embodies idealism and beauty.

During the time of The Lover, we experience new confidence and trust in ourselves. We feel light of heart and joyful, and our inner radiance shines forth and attracts others to us.

"In the early Celtic church, a person who acted as a teacher, companion, or spiritual guide was called an anam cara. It originally referred to someone to whom you confessed, revealing the hidden intimacies of your life. With the anam cara you could share your innermost self, your mind your heart. This friendship was an act of recognition and belonging. When you had an anam cara, your friendship cut across all convention, morality, and category. You were joined in an ancient and eternal way with the 'friend of your soul.'"

—John O'Donohue[61]

LAUGHTER/ JOY

Pleasure. Happiness. Playfulness.
Expansiveness. Dawn. Awakening.
Good fortune. Release from suffering.

"Like two lovers who have become lost
In a winter blizzard

And find a cozy empty hut
In the forest,

I now huddle everywhere
With the Friend.

God and I have built an immense fire
Together.

We keep each other happy
And warm."

—**Hafiz**[62]

The Laughter/Joy card represents a stage in the journey when the hero/heroine has passed through the threshold, has survived the "night-sea" journey and realizes it. It is the moment of release, relief, and awakening. This moment can come in a very simple, quiet way, just as the sun rises with little fanfare in the morning. But the heart feels great joy because the heart feels the Radiance—not as a theory but as an actual experience.

When you pull the Laughter/Joy card, you are being encouraged to recognize your good fortune. Long-awaited results are soon to be yours. If you have been suffering, the pain will be relieved. If you have been joyful, the feeling will grow.

Pulling the Laughter/Joy card indicates sweetness and beauty now in your life.

"I can so easily lean my cheek across this small table
Of time and space

And let you touch my beautiful laughing
Wooly beard.

. . .

My only duty that now remains
To this world

Is from every direction
To forever serve you wine and
Hope"

—**Hafiz**[63]

DANCE/ THE BODY

MOVEMENT. PHYSICAL EXPRESSION OF JOY.
THE CREATION OF JOY THROUGH MOVEMENT.
EXERCISE. RIGHT DIET. GOOD RAPPORT WITH THE EARTH ELEMENT. TRUST IN THE SELF. A STILL CENTER.

"I am a Golden Compass—
Watch me whirl

. . .

In all directions I will true your course
Toward laughter and unity."

—Hafiz[64]

Feeling joy, one cannot help but dance! Dance/The Body is the card of physical movement in a radiant manner. It is the twirling energy of the Sufi dancer who remains securely centered while spinning. Through unself-conscious expression through the body of the powers that lie within, those powers come to the surface and become available for "powering" the dancer's life.

If you have pulled the Dance/The Body card, you are being reminded to include your physical body in your spiritual practice. The Dance/The Body card reminds us not to repress physical expression. The body is the sacred vehicle of earthly life.

Remember to treat your body lovingly and honorably. When we lovingly care for our physical bodies, we are expressing our thankfulness and respect for the life that we have been given.

Dancing is a natural form of expressing joy. It is innate in all human beings. Everyone can dance.

Into every country
I will carry the Holy Names and dance
And dance.

. . .

Watch me whirl into nothingness
Your fears and darkness—
Just keep tossing them onto my golden plate."

—**Hafiz**[65]

SING/ THE VOICE

Self-expression. One's true calling.
Individuation. Poetry. Song.
The music of the spheres. Finding one's voice.
Giving one's gift to the world.

"... for well dear brother I know
If thou wast not granted to sing thou would'st surely die."
—**Walt Whitman**[66]

Sing/The Voice is the card of self-expression—the unfettered, unself-conscious, free-flowing of one's gifts and talents into the world. It is the finding and expressing of one's true calling. Sing/The Voice may be quiet, hidden, hermit-like, and self-fulfilled with no need for recognition from others. Or it may be exuberant and highly visible.

When you pull the Sing/The Voice card, you are being encouraged to give your gift, to trust your own innate capacities and to remember that all things happen in their own way and in their own time, so there is no need to hurry or push.

If you are shy, trust that shyness. It may mean that your gift is like a beautiful flower that needs shade if it is to grow. There is nothing wrong with protection and tenderness toward the self.

The Sing/The Voice card is a promise and a reminder. The world needs your gift. Walk the path joyfully and with gratitude, and your song will be sung.

"Stones are longing for what you know.
. . .
The stones and stars envy the movements
Of your legs and tongue
And call you to sing on their behalf.
. . .
In the hidden choir
God and His friends will forever
Conduct."
—**Hafiz**[67]

THE WISE ONE/ THE GREY ANCIENT

EMBODIED WISDOM. GRANDMOTHER. MERLIN. ELDER. SPIRITUAL TEACHER. COMPLETION.

"He was neither old nor young I saw, but the epithet 'middle-aged' could not possibly apply. 'Timeless' was rather the word. His face was like a landscape ravaged. Dry riverbeds ran from brow to chin; the cheeks were two eroded hillocks; the nose a promontory. And his eyes! Luminous stones, not green, not blue, but turquoise lit from within."

—P. L. Travers[68]

The Wise One represents the actual presence in our lives of a human being who embodies the attributes of a wise grandmother and/or of Merlin. This person may or may not be recognized by us as a guide and carrier of wisdom. It may be someone whose value is not recognized by the community. Often the wise ones are hidden, and we must be spiritually ready ourselves before we can recognize that person.

Pulling The Wise One advises you to look about you for a person in your community who has wisdom and guidance to offer you. You must ask the person before the wisdom or guidance can be received. The act of asking indicates humility and wisdom, and demonstrates your readiness to step forward on your path.

The Wise One also invites you to recognize and tap into this energy in yourself through spiritual practices such as meditation. You are being reminded of your own inner wise guide, and that you, also, are The Wise One.

"The Master sees things as they are,
without trying to control them.
She lets them go their own way,
and resides at the center of the circle."
Tao Te Ching[69]

RETURN

RETURN TO THE COMMUNITY AFTER A LONG SOJOURN IN THE WILDERNESS. THE GIFT. REINCARNATION. THE DRAGONFLY. THE HUMMINGBIRD. ACCEPTING ONE'S RESPONSIBILITY.

"You must return
with the bliss
and integrate it.

. . .

The return is seeing
the radiance everywhere."

—**Joseph Campbell**[70]

Return is the final stage in the hero/heroine's journey and, as such, it is also a beginning. In the archetypal hero's journey, the hero must leave the community and all that is familiar when s/he hears "the call" to activate and realize her or his own unique path. But there comes a stage in the journey when the gift has been won, the song has been heard. The quest is complete.

When this happens, the hero/heroine returns to the community and becomes an elder who can guide others with the gift of wisdom.

Pulling the Return card heralds the beginning of a new life. It is life as an elder and guide who has learned to embody the Radiance and can now share and communicate that gift to others.

Often, the returning hero/heroine is not recognized by the community. He or she may wear no mantle, have no title. Often obscure and engaged in humble tasks, the returned hero or heroine is nonetheless a guide. Those who need guidance may recognize him or her and ask for assistance; or, those who need help may not recognize the elder but may still encounter him/her on their path. If the one who needs help cannot see clearly, the elder will appear as a monster or trickster or will be invisible—the guardian at the gate who must be encountered if the gate is to be passed.

When you pull the Return card, it indicates either that you are an elder, or are about to encounter one, or need to recognize that power in yourself.

At the final stage of physical life, the Return card indicates a return of the soul to the Radiance and the imminent rebirth of that soul in its new form.

The dragonfly and hummingbird are Radiant beings who image forth the spiritual truth of the eventual return of all forms.

"I depart as air, I shake my white locks at the runaway sun,
I effuse my flesh in eddies, and drift it in lacy jags.
I bequeath myself to the dirt to grow from the grass I love,
If you want me again look for me under your boot-soles.

. . .

Failing to fetch me at first keep encouraged,
Missing me one place search another,
I stop somewhere waiting for you."

—**Walt Whitman**[71]

CONCLUSION

"Men need such lively oracles in order to sustain their existence. Lay them to heart, if you will. Even so, we take the road empty-handed, remember, without even a map to guide us; not dreaming that we carry treasure, nor hoping that someone will run to meet us . . . The way itself knows where it is going. The way itself will lift us forward. The way itself is all."

—P. L. Travers[1]

The individual cards of *The WayCard Oracle* when read in succession comprise a circular cycle. This cycle traces the life journey. We begin in the Radiance—a realm of unbounded beauty and possibility. Through the process of incarnation, we come into the physical plane where our bodies are sustained by the elements of Air, Fire, Water, and Earth. We begin as the Child in a condition of innocence and "beginner's mind." Our first earthly home is a Nest that, ideally, offers safety and security. From that place of safety and security, we begin our quest. We become Heroes or Heroines who Travel the Way, the path of pilgrimage. To travel, we must have Willingness—a state of mind and condition of heart supported by courage. One component of our Self that guides us on the journey is the Ego, our personality. This component of the Self is not always clear, as it contains all of the unresolved karma of previous lifetimes. Because of this we sometimes use Force to get what we want. But force is of no effect when we encounter a Threshold.

At the Threshold—a boundary that marks the end of one phase and the beginning of another—guardians appear that block our passage. We may be tempted to use force, but doing so brings unproductive results. At the threshold, we are often seduced by an energy that attracts or repels us. Seduction is a necessary energy that propels us on our journey, activating the ego and embodying the lessons we need to learn. Given the lack of clarity inevitable when we follow fear and desire, after giving in to the allure of seduction, we experience a fall, a Betrayal that leaves us in Tears, often Grieving a very great loss—the loss of an aspect of our innocence, which is also the loss of the illusion that caused us to believe in our desire or to believe in our fear.

Challenging at this phase is the presence of The Judge. When we have experienced a fall, when we are grieving to this degree, we may judge ourselves negatively or blame others. This action of negative judgment must be transformed into the positive force of judgment as discrimination—a capacity to evaluate with reason and clarity of mind.

This capacity of transforming the mind from a negative, judging force to a positive discriminating force can only be wholly attained if we make a positive choice at the Crossroads that now confronts us.

At this Crossroads, we will be offered a number of choices, some or all of which will conflict with each other. In order to discern rightly at this stage, ego must become quiet. All force must be put aside, and we must enter in the Silence.

In the Silence, we can be assisted by Old Knowledge, the repository of the wisdom of the ancients, often available in actual physical form in manuscripts or runic inscriptions. As we delve into Old Knowledge, we now open an Inner Door—the doorway to Initiation.

Here we recognize that our old approaches are no longer working, and we find in ourselves a new capacity to Let Go, to surrender Ego and replace it with Faith. Once we have faith, we can then Focus our minds. We can allow thoughts that impede us to dissipate and thoughts that further our spiritual goals to guide us.

With Faith and Focus come Gratitude, now no longer a concept but a reality. We feel deep in our hearts a "healing fountain"[2] that "blesses unaware."[3] In this now newly healed capacity of heart, for the first time, we also develop the capacity of genuine Forgiveness—forgiveness of the Self for not being perfect—acceptance of our humanity and recognition that in being human we, inevitably, encounter falls. Having learned to forgive ourselves, we now also are able to forgive others and what once seemed a wrong done to us is now perceived with the clarity that Jesus had when he said, "Forgive them they know not what they do."

With forgiveness of self and others, we now encounter Love for the first time. What we had thought to be Love before we now recognize was desire or fear in illusory clothing. But with the capacities of faith, gratitude, and forgiveness, genuine Love becomes possible.

This Love guides us into actions of Reciprocity. We bow to the sacredness of life, to the beauty of each force and being, of each moment and event. We give back to life and in so doing, again for the first time, encounter a genuine Lover—the world gives back to us from a place of genuine Love. Feeling the presence of The Lover, receiving the world embrace, we feel Laughter and Joy.

The Laughter and Joy well up from deep within and inspire us to Dance so that we re-inhabit our Body with great vitality and health. The feeling of being so vitally alive causes us to Sing; our Voice is our gift that we give to the world—whatever energy, talent, or action most suits us now emerges from us unimpeded.

Thus we become The Wise One, The Grey Ancient—Grandmother, Merlin, Giver of Counsel. And in so doing, we experience the hero or heroine's Return to the community. We have fulfilled our quest and can now return to the land we came from with deep, personal power and an abiding sense of our own responsibility to give back to our community.

The cycle of the journey is complete, and when we no longer need our body, we leave the body and return to the Radiance from which we came—and a new cycle begins.

ENDNOTES

Epigraph

1. Matsuo Basho, *Basho's Narrow Road: Spring & Autumn Passages,* Trans. Hiroaki Sato (Berkeley, CA: Stonebridge Press, 2003) 41.

Interpretations *of the* WayCards

1. William Wordsworth, "Ode: Intimations of Immortality," *William Wordsworth: The Poems* (New Haven: Yale University Press, 1977), 525.
2. Eileen Caddy, *Opening Doors Within: 365 Daily Meditations from Findhorn* (Scotland UK: Findhorn Press, 1986), 121.
3. Han-shan, *Cold Mountain,* trans. Burton Watson (New York: Columbia Univ. Press, 1970), 58.
4. Stephen Mitchell, *Tao Te Ching* (NY: HarperPerennial, 1988), 59.
5. Hildegarde of Bingen, quoted in David Suzuki, *The Sacred Balance* (Vancouver: Greystone Books, 2002), 105.
6. Hafiz, *The Subject Tonight is Love: 60 Wild and Sweet Poems of Hafiz,* Versions by Daniel Ladinsky (North Myrtle Beach, SC: Pumpkin House Press, 1997), 43.
7. Masaru Emoto, *The Hidden Messages in Water,* trans. David A. Thayne (Hillsboro, Oregon: Beyond Words Publishing, 2004), 1.
8. *Tao Te Ching,* 78
9. Joan Halifax, *The Fruitful Darkness: Reconnecting with the Body of the Earth* (San Francisco: HarperSanFrancisco, 1993), 52.
10. Stephen Harrod Buhner, *Sacred Plant Medicine: Explorations in the Practice of Indigenous Herbalism* (Boulder, Colorado: Roberts Rhinehart Publishers, 1996), 26.
11. Walt Whitman, "There was a child went forth," *Leaves of Grass* (NY: Modern Library, 2001), 454–55.
12. Angeles Arrien, *The Four-Fold Way* (NY: HarperSanFrancisco, 1993), 21–22.
13. Alexander Carmichael, *Carmina Gadelica: Hymns & Incantations* (Edinburgh: Floris Books, 1992), 63.
14. Joseph Campbell, *Reflections on the Art of Living: A Joseph Campbell Companion,* ed. Diane Osbon (NY: HarperCollins, 1991), 77.
15. *ibid.,* 23.
16. *Tao Te Ching,* 46.
17. Halifax, *The Fruitful Darkness,* 52
18. Campbell, *Reflections on the Art of Living,* 26.
19. *ibid.,* 149.
20. *Tao Te Ching,* 29.
21. Alan Watts, *TAO: The Watercourse Way* (NY: Pantheon Books, 1975), 38.
22. *Tao Te Ching,* 64
23. Campbell, *Reflections on the Art of Living,* 78
24. Halifax, *The Fruitful Darkness,* 26.

25. P. L. Travers, *What the Bee Knows: Reflections on Myth, Symbol, and Story* (London: Arkana, Penguin, 1989), 85.
26. Christina Rossetti, "Goblin Market," *Christina Rossetti: The Complete Poems* (London: Penguin, 2001), 5.
27. Charlotte Bronte, *Jane Eyre* (Pleasantville, NY: Reader's Digest Publishing, 1984, unabridged), 411.
28. Jean Houston, *The Search for the Beloved: Journeys in Mythology and Sacred Psychology* (NY: Tarcher, 1997), 118.
29. Dante Alighieri, *Divine Comedy,* trans. Henry W. Longfellow (Penn State University, http://www2.hn.psu.edu/faculty/jmanis/dante/Dante-Longfellow.pdf, 7).
30. Campbell, *Reflections on the Art of Living,* 152.
31. *ibid.,* 119–20.
32. *ibid.,* 120.
33. *ibid.,* 120
34. Arnold Mindell, *The Shaman's Body: A New Shamanism for Transforming Health, Relationships, and the Community* (NY: HarperCollins, 1993), . 140.
35. Thich Nhat Hanh, *The Miracle of Mindfulness* (Boston: Beacon Press, 1976), 61.
36. Whitman, "Song of the Open Road," 185.
37. *Tao Te Ching,* 15.
38. Halifax, *The Fruitful Darkness,* 24–25.
39. Lakota John Fire Lame Deer, quoted in Halifax, 25.
40. Travers, *What the Bee Knows,* 5.
41. Halifax, *The Fruitful Darkness,* 103.
42. *The Holy Bible,* King James Version (New York: American Bible Society, 1999) Matthew," 7:7-8.
43. Rudolf Steiner, "Autobiograhical Sketch," in *The Essential Steiner: Basic Writings of Rudolf Steiner,* ed Robert A. McDermott (San Francisco: Harper Row, 1984), 14.
44. *Tao Te Ching,* 48.
45. *ibid.,* 37.
46. Chief Seattle's speech as published in 1887. online.sfsu.edu/rone/Environ/Seattle.html.
47. *The Rule of Taize* (NY: Seabury Press, 1968), 43.
48. Leslie Marmon Silko, *Ceremony* (NY: Penguin, 1986), 135.
49. Rudolf Steiner, "The Path of Knowledge," in *The Essential Steiner: Basic Writings of Rudolf Steiner,* ed. Robert A. McDermott (San Francisco: Harper & Row, 1984), 79.
50. Doug Boyd, *Rolling Thunder* (NY: Delta, 1974), 52.
51. Samuel Taylor Coleridge, "The Rhyme of the Ancient Mariner," *The Oxford Book of English Verse, 1250–1918,* ed. Sir Arthur Quiller-Couch (NY: Oxford University Press, 1939), 654–655.
52. Boyd, *Rolling Thunder,* 52.
53. *The Holy Bible,* John 8:7.
54. Jon Kabat-Zinn, *Wherever You Go There You Are: Mindfulness Meditation in Everyday Life* (NY: Hyperion, 1994), 226.

55. John O'Donohue, *Anam Cara: A Book of Celtic Wisdom* (NY: HarperCollins, 1997), 15.
56. *The Rule of Taize,* 127.
57. Barre Toelken, "Seeing with a Native Eye: How Many Sheep Will it Hold?" in *Seeing with a Native Eye: Essays on Native American Religion,* ed Walter Holden Capps (NY: Harper & Row, 1976), 15–17.
58. Boyd, *Rolling Thunder,* 58.
59. *ibid.,* 122.
60. Houston, *The Search for the Beloved,* 235.
61. O'Donohue, *Anam Cara,* 13–14.
62. Hafiz, *The Subject Tonight is Love,* 10.
63. *ibid.,* 39.
64. *ibid.,* 38.
65. *ibid.,* 38.
66. Whitman, "When Lilacs Last in the Dooryard Bloomed," 408.
67. Hafiz, *The Subject Tonight is Love,* 42–43.
68. Travers, *What the Bee Knows,* 108.
69. *Tao Te Ching,* 29.
70. Campbell, *Reflections on the Art of Living,* 290.
71. Whitman, "Song of Myself," 114–15.

Conclusion

1. Travers, *What the Bee Knows,* 155.
2. W. H. Auden, "In Memory of W. B. Yeats," *Another Time* (NY: Faber & Faber; New Edition, 2007), 17–18.
3. Coleridge, "The Rhyme of the Ancient Mariner," 656.

BIBLIOGRAPHY

Alighieri, Dante. *Divine Comedy*, trans. Henry W. Longfellow. Penn State University, www2.hn.psu.edu/faculty/jmanis/dante/Dante-Longfellow.pdf.

Arrien, Angeles. *The Four-Fold Way*. NY: HarperSanFrancisco, 1993.

Auden, W.H. *Another Time*. NY: Faber & Faber; New Edition, 2007.

Basho, Matsuo. *Basho's Narrow Road: Spring & Autumn Passages*, trans. Hiroaki Sato. Berkeley, CA: Stonebridge Press, 2003.

Boyd, Doug. *Rolling Thunder*, NY: Delta, 1974.

Bronte, Charlotte. *Jane Eyre*. Pleasantville, NY: Reader's Digest, 1984, unabridged.

Buhner, Stephen Harrod. *Sacred Plant Medicine: Explorations in the Practice of Indigenous Herbalism*. Boulder, Colorado: Roberts Rhinehart Publishers, 1996.

Caddy, Eileen. *Opening Doors within: 365 Daily Meditations from Findhorn*. Scotland, UK: Findhorn Press, 1986.

Carmichael, Alexander. *Carmina Gadelica: Hymns & Incantations*. Edinburgh: Floris Books, 1992.

Campbell, Joseph. *Reflections on the Art of Living: A Joseph Campbell Companion*, ed. Diane Osbon. NY: HarperCollins, 1991.

Coleridge, Samuel Taylor. "The Rhyme of the Ancient Mariner," *The Oxford Book of English Verse, 1250*

1918, ed. Sir Arthur Quiller-Couch. NY: Oxford University Press, 1939.

Emoto, Masaru. *The Hidden Messages in Water*, trans. David A. Thayne. Hillsboro, Oregon: Beyond Words, 2004.

Hafiz. *The Subject Tonight is Love: 60 Wild and Sweet Poems of Hafiz*, Versions by Daniel Ladinsky. North Myrtle Beach, SC: Pumpkin House, 1997.

Halifax, Joan. *The Fruitful Darkness: Reconnecting with the Body of the Earth*. San Francisco: HarperSanFrancisco, 1993.

Han-shan. *Cold Mountain*, trans. Burton Watson. New York: Columbia University. Press, 1970.

Hanh, Thich Nhat. *The Miracle of Mindfulness*. Boston: Beacon, 1976.

Houston, Jean. *The Search for the Beloved: Journeys in Mythology and Sacred Psychology*. NY: Tarcher, 1997.

Kabat-Zinn, Jon. *Wherever You Go There You Are: Mindfulness Meditation in Everyday Life*. NY: Hyperion, 1994.

Murray, Liz and Colin. *The Celtic Tree Oracle: A System of Divination*. NY: St. Martin's, 1988.

Mindell, Arnold. *The Shaman's Body: A New Shamanism for Transforming Health, Relationships, and the Community*. NY: HarperCollins, 1993.

O'Donohue, John. *Anam Cara: A Book of Celtic Wisdom*. NY: HarperCollins, 1997.

Rossetti, Christina. "Goblin Market," *Christina Rossetti: The Complete Poems*. London: Penguin, 2001.

The Rule of Taize. NY: Seabury, 1968.

Seattle, Chief. Online.sfsu.edu/rone/Environ/Seattle.html.

Silko, Leslie Marmon. *Ceremony*. NY: Penguin, 1986.

Steiner, Rudolf. *The Essential Steiner: Basic Writings of Rudolf Steiner*, ed Robert A. McDermott. San Francisco: Harper Row, 1984.

Suzuki, David. *The Sacred Balance*. Vancouver: Greystone, 2002.

Tao Te Ching. Trans. Stephen Mitchell. NY: HarperPerennial, 1988.

Toelken, Barre. *Seeing with a Native Eye: Essays on Native American Religion*, ed Walter Holden Capps. NY: Harper & Row, 1976.

Travers, P. L. *What the Bee Knows: Reflections on Myth, Symbol, and Story*. London: Arkana, Penguin, 1989.

Watts, Alan. *TAO: The Watercourse Way*. NY: Pantheon, 1975.

Whitman, Walt. *Leaves of Grass*. NY: Modern Library, 2001.

Wordsworth, William. *William Wordsworth: The Poems*. New Haven: Yale University Press, 1977.

Other Schiffer Books on Related Subjects

The I Ching Oracle Wheel: A Divination System
Jim Edward Lucier
ISBN: 978-0-7643-4717-7

Nature's Wisdom Oracle
Mindy Lighthipe
ISBN: 978-0-7643-3573-0